To Sarah
... practice makes perfect!
Love, Marilee

Praise for
101 Simple Ways to Be Good to Yourself

"*The perfect gift—a book to treasure for years and years. It will help people value themselves more and move in a positive direction.***"**

—Judy "JT" Corley
Diamond Sales Director,
Discovery Toys, Inc.

"*Should be read by everyone. It is warm, wonderful, winsome, and full of ideas and tidbits that enhance the quality of your life. I enjoyed every single page!***"**

—Brian Tracy
President, Brian Tracy Learning Systems

"*A breath of fresh air. A winner for sure! Full of super ideas. I appreciate the light, bubbly quality.***"**

—Barbara Johnson
Director, Spatula Ministries
Author of *Splashes of Joy in the Cesspool of Life*

"*Exceptional! Required reading for any young person who wants to excel in their personal and career life—and for anyone who wants to live life to the fullest.***"**

—Mark R. Truitt
Executive Director,
National Seminars Group

101 SIMPLE WAYS TO BE *Good* TO YOURSELF

Donna Watson

To my Dad,
a very special man

101 SIMPLE WAYS TO BE Good TO YOURSELF

How to Discover Peace and Joy in Your Life

Donna Watson, Ph.D.

A BARD PRODUCTIONS BOOK

ENERGY PRESS

For information about quantity purchases contact:

Energy Press
5275 McCormick Mountain Drive
Austin, Texas 78734
512-266-2112 Phone
512-266-2749 FAX

Paperback edition: ISBN 0-9631195-0-8

Hardcover edition: ISBN 0-9631195-2-4

A BARD PRODUCTIONS BOOK
AUSTIN, TEXAS

Copyediting: **Helen Hyams**

Text Design: **Suzanne Pustejovsky**

Jacket/Cover Design: **Suzanne Pustejovsky**

Composition/Production: **Round Rock Graphics**

CONTENTS

THE AUTHOR

Donna Watson is an energizer. Her ever-optimistic attitude and hard work have enabled her to overcome many of life's challenges and to assist others in changing their lives for the better. Each year she crisscrosses the country and travels internationally, speaking to thousands. Her audiences gain a wealth of practical life-enriching techniques, common sense, and inspiration.

Donna has been a sixth-grade teacher, legal secretary, manager of a farm equipment company, executive director of a large private nonprofit corporation, direct sales manager, radio show host, and owner of her own consulting firm. Her undergraduate degree is in education; her M.B.A. and Ph.D. degrees are in management. Her doctoral studies addressed practical techniques to reduce stress.

Donna and her husband Robert live in Oklahoma City. Her three daughters and their families—Kristie and Stephen and grandson Kristopher, Jennifer and Tyler, and Tracey—live nearby. When not on the road speaking, Donna enjoys spending time with family and friends, painting, sewing, and doing community work.

◇

INTRODUCTION

Sometimes we get so busy that we forget to notice what a beautiful world we live in. We don't notice the smile of a child, the leaves turning gold and red, or a rainbow promising hope. We miss hearing the laughter off in the distance or seeing the sun sparkle across the water. We fail to notice how warm it makes us feel inside when we better someone's day. We forget to make our memories.

Memories come from the simple things in life. The smile, the laughter, the thought—these are the ways we make our memories. This is how we are good to ourselves. This is what makes life worth living.

Join me now as we go through an assortment of the things that make life worth living—the simple ways to be good to yourself. Some may be things that you are already doing. Others are ideas you may have heard in the past and forgotten; maybe I can remind you to try them again. And some may be new ideas you would like to try for the first time. Pick and choose the ones that suit you the best. Maybe you can try

◇

one or two now, then come back later and try a few more. You are a wonderfully unique and very special person and the ideas you choose are special because you are.

   Someone once said, "I did not come to teach, I came to remind." And that is my reason for writing this book—to remind you what a beautiful world you live in and to encourage you to be good to yourself as you enjoy it.

   God bless you,

Donna

Donna

BELIEVE IN YOU

Believe in you because you are unique. You can do things no one else can do. You can be things no one else can be. You touch the lives of other people in a way that only you can. You are a blessing to this world.

You have a right to be here because you are very special. You are here for an important reason. Your purpose in this world can be fulfilled by no one else.

Sometimes people and circumstances cause us to doubt our importance. Please, don't ever let that happen to you. Believe in you because you have a right to. If for some reason you can't believe in you right now, then let me believe in you until you can believe in you. It would be my privilege.

DON'T "SHOULD"

*D*on't let anyone "should" on you. Don't we do that? Then, when other people get through "should-ing" on us, we "should" on ourselves. What happens next? If we don't do all of those "shoulds," we feel guilty!

Do you know what guilt is? It is nothing more than excess emotional baggage. Guilt is a lot like worry, and worry is like sitting in a rocking chair: it gives you something to do but it doesn't take you anywhere.

We have a right to make choices in our lives and sometimes the "shoulds" may not be the right choice for us at the present moment. Be your own person. Don't let the "shoulds" control your life.

MAGICAL MUSIC

Make some time to listen to music. Don't watch TV, pay the bills, and read at the same time. Just listen to music.

Sit in a comfortable chair or lie on the sofa and turn down the lights. You may even want to light a candle and watch the flames dance to the music.

Music can create magic in our lives.

OWN YOUR TELEPHONE

*H*ow many times have you made a mad dash across your yard, your house, or your workplace to catch the telephone? Who owns that telephone? Maybe in the workplace that mad dash is necessary, but at home the telephone belongs to you. If you don't want to answer it, let it ring. The world won't come to an end. If the call is really that urgent, the other person will call back. You own your telephone. It does not own you.

A PLANT FOR A LONELY ROOM

After my daughter married, I suddenly discovered that I had difficulty going into her room. There were so many memories in there. Things that had happened in the past would never happen in just that way again. I knew she was happy and where she wanted to be and should be. For that I was delighted. But things were different and that room represented a part of our relationship that would never be again.

So one day I went out and bought a great big ivy and a beautiful pot to put it in. Her room is at the end of the hall and I put that ivy on a bookcase just inside the room so that I could see it every time I walked down the hall. It has to be watered. I am the only one in our family who waters plants. I am needed in that room. I have a reason to be there.

We all need to be needed.

MAKE A
"DREAM BOOK"

A friend of mine was telling me of a time in her life when things were just not going well. She decided one day to make a "dream book." She put a picture of a handsome man in there . . . the man of her dreams. She loves diamonds, so she put lots of pictures of diamonds in her book. She had always wanted to go to Bermuda, so she found some pictures of Bermuda and added them to her book. Those were her dreams.

Interestingly enough, she has met the man of her dreams. He is very wealthy and has given her a lot of diamonds. He came in a couple of days before their wedding and said, "I have a great idea for our honeymoon!" You guessed it—Bermuda.

Build a dream book with all your best dreams. Put pictures in it of the life scenes you would like to be in and special places you would like to visit. Include pictures of your ideal home, a beautiful garden—your favorite spot to relax and be you.

Dreams don't always come true. But they might. What have you got to lose?

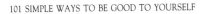

7

TOUCH THE EARTH

*P*lant some flowers in your flower bed or window box. Improve the beauty in your world. Dig in the dirt. Let the soft, moist soil run through your fingers. There is something very peaceful about working with the earth.

I used to tease my dad when I was a kid that he would mow the grass, then sit in the yard and watch it grow. Now I know it was just a peaceful and quiet place for him.

INNER STRENGTH

 *U*se the spiritual resources that are special to you. That may mean prayer, meditation, study, or sharing. You may find a unique strength that is not available through any other source.

9

THE CHOICE IS OURS

One of the greatest blessings we have been given in life is the right to make choices. We have the choice to think, to speak, to act, to behave, and to believe as we choose. Everything we do is a choice, even not making a decision.

One of the things that increases our stress level the most is the feeling of being out of control of our life. The way we stay in control is through our choices. We can choose to stay in a situation, or we can choose to walk away; the choice is always ours. But regardless of the choice, by virtue of the fact that we have made a choice— no matter what it is—we have put ourselves back in control. The choice reduces our stress, because we are being good to ourselves.

HUG YOURSELF

*H*as anyone told you lately that you are doing a great job? You need to hear that. Reach around right now, pat yourself on the back, and say, "You're doing a great job!" Pat both shoulders; it is very good exercise.

When my children were small, I told them that when they needed a hug, all they had to do was run up to us and say, "I haven't had my fourteen hugs today." We would grab each other, quickly squeeze, and recite: "1, 2, 3, 4, 5, 6, 7, 8, 9, 10, 11, 12, 13, 14." They would then be okay and run off to play. You see, I couldn't read their minds and know when they needed that special attention, so we made a game out of it.

Adults need special attention, too. Maybe someone you know needs fourteen hugs today. Maybe it is you.

DON'T "AWFULIZE"

Have you ever "awful-ized"? You know the routine. You are running late in the morning and you think, "I'm running late. I'll probably hit major traffic. If I hit major traffic, I'll probably be late to work. If I am late to work, my boss will be mad at me. If my boss gets mad at me, I'll probably lose my job. If I lose my job, I won't be able to pay my bills. If I can't pay my bills, I'll probably lose my home. If I lose my home, I won't have anyplace to live. If I don't have anyplace to live, I'll probably starve. If I starve, I'll probably die. All because I am running late!"

Really!

DAYDREAM

*T*ake a moment now and then and have a daydream. Dream about some place where you had a wonderful time. Dream about an event that was very special in your life. Dream about something that you very much want to have happen. Visualize it in the greatest of detail—the colors, the sounds, the smells, the sights—exactly as you wish it to happen.

Go through some old pictures and put a collection of them on a bedside table or your dressing table or in your work area. Take the time to look at each of those pictures and remember the happy moments when they were made.

Daydreaming is a great way to take a mini-vacation.

13

EAT THAT BROWNIE!

Diets and cholesterol;
that is all we talk
about. Go to a party and that is
all you will hear. "What are you
doing to lose that extra weight
before the holidays?" "What are
you doing to get ready for the
new summer swimsuits?" "My
doctor has me on this new diet;
you should try it! It's terrific!"

I don't know about you,
but sometimes I get so tired of
hearing this. Sure, my body
doesn't look the way it did when
I was twenty. But then I am not
twenty. (Thank goodness!)

Today is the best day of my
life and I don't want to redo any
of it! I also don't want to spend
the rest of my life fretting about
every morsel I put into my
mouth. This does not mean that
I am not careful. I am careful and
I am very aware of my health,
but sometimes we just gotta let
go and eat that brownie!

BE A KID AGAIN

*D*o you ever wish you could just be a kid again? Not the know-it-all, I-want-my-way child, but the carefree, happy-go-lucky child. You can. Sometimes as adults we are so afraid someone is going to "see us" that we forget how to enjoy and just be.

How long has it been since you went wading? How about running through or playing in a sprinkler? Go out, find a pile of dried leaves, and listen to them crunch as you walk through them. Walk barefoot on grass that is still covered with early-morning dew. Go to the beach and build a castle in the sand.

For one day, leave your inhibitions behind and be a child again. You may find it to be one of the most enjoyable days of your life.

LET IT GO

*T*his is one of my very favorite prayers. Maybe you'll enjoy it too.

SERENITY PRAYER

Grant me the serenity
to accept the things I
cannot change, the courage
to change the things
I can, and the wisdom
to know the difference.

This prayer helps me know when I have done everything about a situation that I possibly can and it is time to let it go.

Sometimes the most effective thing you can do about a situation is to just let it go. I know that is not easy, but sometimes it is necessary. We need to back away and say, "What have I done about this situation so far? Is there anything else I could do about it?"

If there is, then do it. If there is not, then let it go. Worry never accomplished anything worthwhile.

16

SMILES ARE CONTAGIOUS

Smiling is the same in any language. It always means "I'm happy. I care about you." Laughter is a form of internal jogging. It is not only enjoyable; it is also very healthy for you.

Studies are showing that laughter, smiling, and euphoric feelings can actually enhance your immune system and make you healthier.

Laughter is the number one most effective way to deal with stress. Sometimes we have to fake it until we make it. If you act happy, you will begin to feel happy.

Smiles and laughter are very contagious. Share them with a friend.

DO IT NOW

*D*o something you have always wanted to do. Be sure it is legal and moral. If not, that could stress you out!

What have you always wanted to try that you have never allowed yourself to do because it was reckless, or too expensive, or maybe because someone like you just doesn't do that sort of thing? Maybe it is time to make plans to enjoy life a little. How about a ride in a hot-air balloon or a bicycle trip through the Rockies? Why don't you borrow the money and make that long-dreamed trip to Europe? The memories you have while repaying the loan will make it all worthwhile.

As I travel around the world on speaking tours, I see too many women traveling alone on those trips they and their spouses always planned to take, but never got around to. Don't let that be you. Do it now.

JUST BE YOU

Do you ever compare yourself to someone else? Do you say, "If I could just make presentations like Tom," or "If I could only be as much in control as Sarita"? "If." What a big word. What an unnecessary word.

You don't have to be anybody else. Just be you. Be the best you can be. That is the ultimate. We don't want to be a second-rate anyone else. Sure, those other people have special talents and abilities, and there is nothing wrong with us admiring them and learning and growing, but don't imitate. You have special talents and abilities, too. Someone else is probably admiring you. We are all someone else's excellent person. We watch others and others watch us. This is how we learn and grow.

TIME TO UNWIND

*H*ave you ever had a day full of crises only to come home at night and meet another mountain of crises? Sure, we all have. But what happens when you have not put yourself back together between those times? That's right. That mountain of crises can turn into a volcano!

Set aside time to unwind. Maybe you need to hire the babysitter for an extra half-hour and spend that time in the park on the way home just meditating, or being quiet, or simply looking at the beautiful world around you.

Maybe you need to set aside time when you first get home that is just for you . . . transition time. Let everyone know that you will fulfill all those wants and needs if you are allowed thirty minutes to put yourself back together again.

A SENSE OF BALANCE

Are you on the fast track of life, trying to fulfill all those "Superperson" requirements? Good luck!

In case you haven't figured it out, it won't work. We are human beings. We are not "super-beings." Personally, I think that is okay. It means I am not expected to be perfect. What a relief!

But I do have to keep a sense of balance in my life. That's not always easy, but it is necessary. I know other people watch me. My children do and I am setting an example for them. I don't want them to become workaholics. I want them to know the importance of play.

Set aside specific times to work and specific times to play. You must have both. If you can't do what you enjoy, then enjoy what you do. But keep your life in balance.

No Pity Parties!

No pity parties allowed! That's right! We shouldn't have them at all, but if you just have to have one, remember the rules: only one a week and only for fifteen minutes. Enjoy it because you are only allowed one.

Put on some sad music and really get with it. Cry. Feel sorry for yourself. Review all the sad situations you can come up with. But be sure to set a timer, because when fifteen minutes have passed, you are through and you can't have another one until the same time next week.

PUT IT AWAY

Have you noticed that sometimes things have to be said to you over and over again before they sink in? That's the way I was about this saying— "Don't put it down; put it away." I had read it so many times and had thought about it, but one day it really stuck. I thought, "That makes so much sense! If you don't have time to put it away now, you probably won't have time to put it away later."

Think about it. When you walk into your home at night with an armful of stuff, what do you do with it? Dump it, right? Why don't you dump it where it belongs right then and save yourself a lot of time?

Be good to you!

UNPLAN AN EVENING

*D*o you ever get the feeling that you run all the time? Sometimes we get on the fast track, overloading on activities. This happens to both single people and those who are married. For singles it turns out to be a meeting, a party, an activity, a sport, a friendship. For married people with children it is a piano lesson, a soccer game, a tennis match, a dance lesson, a scout meeting. We end up on the fast track of time.

Whoa! Let's back off. Set aside one evening a week that is totally unplanned, time when you and the significant people in your world can do anything you want to, maybe even be alone. As one of my sixth-grade students told me, "Try it, you might like it!"

TALENTS

What are you good at? I mean really good at. I'm not talking about golf or fishing or hunting or bicycling. What about building friendships? Maybe you are creative or good at analysis. Maybe you are a peacemaker. Maybe you make other people feel good about themselves.

Make a list. Post it where you can see it first thing every morning. Put it on your bathroom mirror. Recognize your unique talents and abilities. Start the day knowing how special you are.

MILLIONS OF MARBLES

A very successful executive I know has a collection of fishbowls in her office that are full of marbles. When she does something she is proud of or just feels good about, she puts a marble in the fishbowl. Then, if a day comes along with a negative experience, a quick glance at all the marbles in the fishbowls reassures her that most of the time success prevails. (She never takes a marble out!)

At the end of your day try making an "Accomplishments" list. Write down all the things you accomplished—thirteen emergencies, sixteen phone calls, three contracts, and one successful negotiation. Maybe you never got to your "To-Do" list, but you had a successful day.

P.S.: This works in your personal life just as well as it does in your professional life.

"WISH BANK"

*F*ind a special box or jar and create a "wish bank" for yourself. Make a list of things you would like to do but just never seem to get around to. Put some five-minute items in there. Add some ten-minute items or maybe some fifteen- or thirty-minute items.

Then periodically grant yourself a wish. Draw out a wish card and make it come true. Maybe this one says, "I wish I had thirty minutes to read a good book." Do it!

LITTLE THINGS

What goes around, comes around. When you are kind to other people they will be kind to you.

Do and say nice things for those significant people in your world. Buy a mini-gift once in a while for no reason at all. It might just be a favorite candy bar or a sweet roll. Go out of your way to pick up someone's dry cleaning when you know that person has a particularly busy day. Stop in the middle of a conversation and tell people how handsome or how beautiful they look today. Call when you are on the way to meet them and let them know it will be 17½ minutes until you arrive. Share a sunset.

It's the little things that count. When you give to others, you feel as if you have given to yourself.

28

KNOCK

When you are bored or feeling left out, go where the action is.

I hear people say, "Nothing exciting ever happens in my life." Maybe you are the one who has to make the excitement. Maybe you are the one who needs to create the fun.

People and activities don't always knock on your door. Sometimes you have to knock on their door.

Take the first step. Get involved!

FUN WITH A SPECIAL FRIEND

Do something enjoyable with the special people in your world at least twice a month. Remember to smile, laugh, have fun, and enjoy life with each other. Sure, life has challenges, but that is not going to change. I think you will find, however, that they are a lot easier to deal with if you try to have a little fun along the way.

So set aside time to have fun. Go to a ball game, a concert, the theater, or a movie. Share dinner with friends. Go antiquing on a Saturday morning. Play golf together (or at least ride while your friend plays). Set aside specific time for each other. If you don't, other "things" will fill that schedule and one day that friendship may be gone.

TIME FOR YOU

o you ever take time for you? I mean really take time for you. What do you do?

I once asked a young mother to do something for herself before she came back for our next counseling session. When she returned I asked her what she had done for herself and she said, "Oh, I took the kids shopping." That is not exactly what I had in mind.

Take an afternoon off to go fishing. Lay in the sun and read a good book. Have your nails done professionally. Have lunch in a quiet corner of a cozy little restaurant. Spend some time in solitude. Give yourself a chance to put yourself back together again. Create what is special for you and do it!

31

KIDNAP!

When was the last time you did something wild and crazy like kidnapping that significant person in your world and going for a picnic in the park? That's too long. How about a special candle-light dinner for two? Decorate your home or work area for Valentine's Day. Put a giant Valentine on the door for that significant person. Celebrate the twelve days of Christmas with a mini-gift exchange each evening. Have a "Because It's Tuesday" party. Send flowers and a love note to that special person in your life. You may be surprised how much they are appreciated. Greet each other at the door the way you did when you first met.

Life does not have to get dull. Be creative!

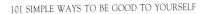

THE GIFT OF TIME

*T*he greatest gift you can give to anyone, including yourself, is the gift of time. Time is a universal gift to each of us every day. We all receive 86,400 seconds a day. We either use them or lose them. Because time is so precious and cannot be expanded, when we share it with someone else we give them a rare and beautiful gift.

Share your time with someone wonderful in your life. Let that person know how important he or she is to your world.

No More "Problems"

Several years ago my husband and I decided that we didn't particularly enjoy having problems. Maybe you are turned on by problems, but they never did a thing for me. Envision someone calling you and saying, "Just wait until you get home tonight. You won't believe the problems that have piled up around here!" That's exciting, isn't it? It becomes a rain cloud that moves over your head and stays all day.

But what about challenges? You can get your teeth into challenges. You can have fun with them. So we decided that from that point on in our lives we just wouldn't have any more problems, only challenges. We just took the word *problem* out of our vocabulary and replaced it with the word *challenge*. Life became a lot more bearable.

Make Time for Yourself

*G*ive yourself fifteen minutes a day that belong to no one but you. Now, that is not much time. Get up fifteen minutes earlier. Stay up fifteen minutes later. Take it out of your lunch hour. Do anything you have to do, but get it.

Do anything you want to do with it. Stand at the window and stare at the trees. Read a good book. Go walking. Sit in the corner and twiddle your thumbs. You see, it really doesn't matter what you do with that time. It's okay to stand at the window and stare at the trees. Just be sure you understand that it's *your* fifteen minutes to stare at trees. That's a gift of time you gave yourself today.

35

MINI-VACATION

Maybe right now your mind and body are saying, "I need a vacation. Let's go to Hawaii and relax!" I'm sold! But maybe you can't take a vacation right now. However, you might take a mini-vacation this weekend. What do you do when you take a mini-vacation? Don't you wait until Sunday night to do the laundry and the shopping and the errands? Okay, so you are going to wait until Sunday night to do the laundry and the shopping and the errands.

Call a friend and work together on your boat. Go window shopping. Take a walk in the woods. Browse through a bookstore. Go on a long, leisurely drive. Remember to have fun. Also remember that fun does not have to be expensive.

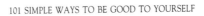

AN ORIGINAL
ARTWORK

I'm an artist. I do oil paintings. No one has ever paid ten thousand dollars for one, but they are my best and they are originals. I'm not a Harriet Beecher Stowe or a Mozart or an Abraham Lincoln, but I give the world my best and I am an original.

Someone said that we are special because the Lord didn't have time to make any junk. He made me special. He made you special. He asked us to do the best with what we have. He never asked us to be perfect. He doesn't expect us to be perfect. He just asked us to be the best original work of art we can be. That's enough.

WHAT'S INSIDE
REALLY COUNTS

*H*ave you ever jumped out of the shower, caught an accidental glimpse of yourself in the mirror, and thought, "Oh my goodness, I must have had a stroke. I know I've had a stroke. I couldn't look this bad otherwise. I've been so busy that no one has had time to tell me."

No, my body doesn't belong to Raquel Welch. My eyes don't belong to Elizabeth Taylor. My legs don't match Lana Turner's. But then, they never did. They are mine, for better or for worse. It's nice to have a body, but what really counts is what is inside. (What a blessing!)

38

REMEMBER TO PLAY

Are you a workaholic? Some people have been raised that way. If you are one of those people, you may have to remember to play. One way is to highlight playtime in yellow on your calendar.

If you need to do this, you probably also need to learn to respect your playtime. We sometimes have to learn to give playtime the same amount of respect we give to business meetings and appointments. Work is essential in our life. So is play.

STEPPING-STONES

See failures as experiences instead of roadblocks. Use them as stepping-stones. When you have a failure, you are not falling backward; you are falling forward. Look at the situation as another experience that can help you grow. Some of the most successful people in the world are those who have failed the most. They were not afraid to face each failure and count it as another stepping-stone, another experience on their road to success.

RITUALS AND
TRADITIONS

A couple of years ago, right before Easter, I decided to give my daughters money for new Easter dresses. They are all grown and I thought they would like to have new Easter dresses. A couple of days after Easter one of my daughters was talking to a friend, knowing that Mother was there listening, and she said, "We had a great time this weekend. We were all home, had new dresses, went out to dinner together, and had a wonderful visit. But we didn't get any Easter baskets." She went ahead to say, "In the past Mother always made us Easter baskets. They always had a little bunny or a hat or a purse, something that she made for us. But this year we didn't get any baskets."

A couple of days later I was talking with a friend of mine, and she said, "Oh yes, I made Easter baskets for everyone this year. I made them for my mother, my mother-in-law, and all three of our boys. Our oldest son is engaged, you know, so I made one for him and his fiancée." She continued, "My son took me in the bedroom and said, 'Mom, do I have to share one with her?'" He was just a senior in dental school that year!

Sometimes we get so busy that we have a tendency to walk away from the rituals and traditions that are so important to the wonderful people in our world. If you are that busy, you are too busy. What's more important than all those special people? Why are we working anyway?

I promise you my kids had Easter baskets last year. In fact, my grandson had one too, and he hadn't even been born. I'm not going to get behind again!

SEND YOURSELF FLOWERS

Remember the card when you send yourself flowers. Write a very special message on it and sign it "An Admirer." Be sure to carefully read it and share it when it arrives in your work area. It will do great things for your popularity that day and wonderful things for your personal morale.

I gave myself a beautiful potted plant years ago on Valentine's Day when I knew that I would not get a present from anyone else. I still have that plant and I have special memories every time I look at it. It reminds me that even though there was no significant person in my life that year, I cared, and I was and am important. So are YOU.

FORGIVE YOURSELF

I work with thousands of people all over the world each year, and I have determined that the majority of them are kind, loving, and forgiving people. If you make a mistake and sincerely ask for forgiveness, not only will most people forgive; they will also forget. They graciously give this gift to all but one person. Who? You're right. Themselves. Don't we deserve the graciousness of forgiveness for ourselves that we extend to others?

Sure, we make mistakes. That just means we are human. We need to look at those mistakes, learn from them, forgive, forget, and move on. We cannot go through life with a gunnysack of guilt draped on our back.

FORGIVE

FORGET

MOVE ON

DON'T EXPECT MIND READING

hen I was working on my doctoral dissertation I had two teenagers living at home. Sometimes I had to go to them and say, "Hey, gang, I really need your help right now." It wasn't that they didn't want to help. They just didn't think about it. They couldn't read my mind.

Sometimes we have bad days. Have you ever noticed that? Maybe when we have one of those bad days we need to go to a friend and say, "Tell me I'm good. Tell me I'm okay." Our friends love us and want to support us, but they can't read our mind. They don't always know when we need that kind of support.

We can't be angry with the special people in our world for not supporting us if they don't know we need support. We can't expect them to read our mind. Sometimes we have to let people know what we need. It's called *communication*.

DANCE

ance. Dance by yourself. Dance with someone else. It is a wonderful way to relax and a great way to exercise. If you hate to exercise, put on some jazz and do your own interpretive dancing. You'll love it!

LOST IN ANOTHER WORLD

Read a novel once in a while, just for fun. Not a self-help book, a novel. Let your mind wander. Relax and have a good time.

Lie back in a hammock and sip lemonade between your naps. Let the world go by.

Enjoy!

PAT A CAT

*P*at a purring cat or a snoozing dog. Animals are known to help lower our blood pressure, literally. A great deal of research is being done now on the positive effects of animals in nursing homes. And case studies exist in which autistic people have been heard speaking to animals when they have not spoken to a human being in years. Animals can be a great source of relaxation and stress reduction. Besides, they feel good.

47

FRIENDS ARE
BLESSINGS

*F*riends are not a luxury;
they are a necessity.
We need them to maintain our
mental and physical well-being.
Personal and professional friendships have to be cultivated and
yet sometimes we get so busy
that days and weeks go by without a contact.

Call someone for lunch
today—even if you only have
fifteen minutes to run to
McDonald's. It doesn't have
to be a two-hour lunch. A
few minutes will do.

Lunch schedule too busy?
Then how about breakfast?
Sometimes I catch someone for
a quick 7:00 A.M. breakfast so
we can still stay in touch and
maintain our busy schedules.

Friends are great blessings.
Don't neglect them.

Go Walking—Fast

One morning as I was working on this book, I got bogged down and my husband suggested I go walking. I said, "I don't have time." He said, "Walk fast!"

I did and I saw beautiful flowers. I saw fall leaves floating down from the trees. I watched my dog run in and out of the yards and play tag with the cars. I took deep breaths, cleared my brain, and wrote the introduction to this book in my mind.

He was right. Even when we don't think we have time to take a break, we need to. Go walking, even if you have to walk fast.

49

SING A
FAVORITE SONG

oesn't it make you feel good to sing a favorite song? It doesn't matter if you can sing or not. Everyone can sing in the shower. It is very difficult to be depressed or unhappy when you are singing! Remember, we don't sing because we are happy. We are happy because we sing.

The same is true of a smile. Look in the mirror and make yourself smile. It is hard to be unhappy when that face in the mirror is smiling back at you.

FEEL-GOOD CLOTHES

Don't we love to wear the clothes that make us feel good? Certain outfits make us feel so spiffy that we're on top of the world. Now we all have clothes in our closet that we don't like. You know, things that we put on and take off or never wear at all. Why don't you get rid of them? You are not going to wear them anyway.

Wear clothes that make you feel good. Buy clothes that are comfortable. Seek out the ones that are easy to maintain and that blend well with what you already have.

Be good to yourself. The way you look can have a direct effect on your attitude for the day.

RESPONSIBLE FOR ME

Sometimes we try to take on the whole world. "I am responsible for my neighbors, my friends, my co-workers, my family—everyone I meet—and if I am not responsible for them, I am letting them down."

Uh uh! We are ultimately responsible for only one person. I am responsible for me. You are responsible for you. Of course, as a parent I am responsible for helping my children grow up and be responsible for themselves, but I do not have to be responsible for the whole world. (Thank goodness!)

MINI-MINI-VACATIONS

*T*ake a mini-mini-
vacation every four to
five hours during the day. That's
right, every four to five hours
during the day. It is really easy
to do this. All you have to do is
get up, walk around, look out
the window, daydream for a few
minutes, or get a drink of water.
Call a travel agency and ask
about a vacation you can't
afford. Do whatever you want
to do. The purpose is to move
yourself around both mentally
and physically for just a few
minutes. You'll love it.

HAPPY TIMES

Sometimes it is easy to forget that there really were happy times. We need to remind ourselves of that periodically. In most of our lives there have been more happy times than sad ones, and yet sometimes they are difficult to remember.

We have the same reaction to criticism. I can go to a seminar with 200 people and have 198 of them write evaluations that say, "What a wonderful seminar! You did an excellent job. I grew so much." Two people out of the 200 will write an evaluation that says, "Bah, humbug."

Which evaluations do I remember? Sure! It is human nature and we have to fight against it every single day. We have to consciously think about those happy times in our lives. It *is* worth the effort.

54

ON THE ROCKS

*T*ry a tall glass of orange juice on the rocks. It is so refreshing! If you don't like orange juice, try tomato juice, grapefruit juice, cranberry juice, or anything else that is good for you . . . but try it on the rocks.

Try it in a crystal glass. It feels even more special that way. Sit back, sip, and enjoy.

DRIVE

*T*ake a long ride on a road that you have never traveled before. Just get out and drive. Relax and forget everything else. When my kids were growing up and I had a particularly stressful day, I would wait for my husband to come home in the evening, and then I would sometimes get in the car by myself and just drive. The solitude, the quiet, and the peace were my way of restoring myself. Maybe it will work for you, too.

SHARE YOUR CHALLENGES

Don't keep your challenges inside. It helps if you share your worries and concerns with someone else. I know this is hard to do sometimes. Private people have a tendency when someone says, "Are you okay?" to reply, "Of course. I'm fine."

When she was a teenager, my daughter was missing for thirteen months. Part of that time we did not know where she was. I was a very private person. One day a friend said to me, "Donna, talk to somebody." I thought, "What is she talking about? I am a professional speaker. I talk to people all day, every day. What does she mean, 'talk to somebody'?" I began to think about what she said and I thought, "You know, she is right. I have got to talk to somebody."

I began to talk to everybody I could find. I would talk to

strangers and to friends. I would say, "Have you got fifteen minutes? Have you got five minutes? I want to talk to you." A very interesting thing happened. I finally got to the point where I could share that information in public, and I had so many people come to me and say, "I didn't know anyone else knew how that felt. I didn't know anyone else knew what that meant. Thank you for sharing that part of your life with us." It's so nice to know that we are not alone and that we can listen and share and grow and restore and recover with others.

My daughter is home now. She is fine. She is beautiful, she is happy, and she likes herself, and I think that is the most important thing that came out of all this. I look back now and I am not sure I could have survived without a very dear friend who told me to talk to somebody.

Sharing can become not only a blessing to you but to other people as well.

TALK LESS AND LISTEN MORE

*I*t is said that the good Lord gave us two ears and one mouth. Maybe that means we need to listen twice as much as we talk. It is worth thinking about, isn't it? You may hear something very interesting.

AVOID CROWDS

Shop in off-hours and on off-days. Go to the bank during times when there are no crowds, maybe early in the morning rather than in the afternoon. Grocery stores are frequently open twenty-four hours a day. I have been known to buy my groceries at two o'clock in the morning. Actually, because there were very few people in the store, it was quite a pleasant experience.

Shopping either early in the morning or late at night rather than during the traditional Saturday and Sunday rush can be much more pleasant for you.

USE YOUR SENSES

My daughter is teaching my grandson, Kristopher, how to use all his senses. It is so much fun to relearn with him. He loves to feel the difference between rock and glass or leaves and a tree trunk. He wants to smell everything and can stay fascinated for minutes at a time with the movement of an ant or a beetle. His ears are so keen. He never misses a bird and runs to the window to see if he can find the sounds of the night.

I love to watch him and see the world through his senses. It's like being in a brand-new world again. Even a meal can be exciting. Most of us just eat. He tastes and oh, the contortions of his face!

Wake up your senses and enjoy the world!

RULED BY THE CLOCK?

Don't let the clock be the tyrant that rules your life. Check your time each day for time wasters. What is wasting your time? Maybe you are talking on the phone too much. Maybe you are watching too much TV or reading too many magazines. Maybe you are allowing more time than you need for appointments.

Set your schedule so that you can handle interruptions or the inevitable delays that come along. Do a time log and find out how long it takes for a particular set of interruptions or phone calls, so that you can make time work for you. Pace yourself. Try to spread out difficult appointments, projects, and even big changes. That is not always possible, but do the best you can.

Learn to guide your life toward peace, not pressure.

61

SAY NO

I have a wonderful sign in my office. You will love it! It says, "WHAT PART OF NO DO YOU NOT UNDERSTAND?" Isn't that terrific? Sometimes we have to learn how to say no to the extra projects, the social events, and the invitations we just don't have the time or energy for. It takes practice, self-respect, and a belief that everyone, every day, needs quiet time to relax and to be alone.

Sometimes it is very difficult to say no to people, but when I say yes to too many projects, then can't get them done, I am not only being unfair to myself; I am also being unfair to the person to whom I made the promise. We need to learn how and when to say no, particularly in our personal lives.

FANTASY LAND

*T*ake five minutes, lean back, and have a marvelous fantasy about yourself. Oh, that is so much fun! What would you really like to be doing if there were no limitations on your world whatsoever? No money limitations, no time limitations, no talent limitations . . . What would you love to be doing? Enjoy the fantasy.

Author and lecturer Napoleon Hill said, "What the mind of man can conceive and believe, the mind of man can achieve." Maybe that fantasy can become a reality.

WEEKEND GETAWAY

*P*lan regular times away from home. If you have children, get a sitter once in a while. You don't have to go anywhere expensive or a long way from home. One of the things my husband did for me when the children were small was that on Valentine's Day each year he hired someone to take care of the children and whisked me off to the local Holidome for the weekend. The first time, it had been unusually cold and icy and we both had a bad case of cabin fever. When we walked into that beautiful place we found green trees and warm moisture in the air. There was a swimming pool, a sauna, and a room where one could take a sunbath. It was my joy, my rejuvenation, for the winter. That weekend helped me sur-vive the rest of the winter.

Those little weekends away can make a lot of difference. If you can't get away for a whole weekend, try just one afternoon. Sometimes we have to back off and restore.

Marriage partners can easily grow apart when they are raising children. They get so busy with activities and errands and jobs and all the daily challenges that they begin to wander in different directions. It does not take a great deal of time to stay in touch, but it does take effort. It is something we have to give to our relationships if they are important enough for us to keep them going. Nothing is quite as scary as having all your children grow up and leave home, and suddenly realizing that you are alone in the house with a stranger.

RENEW OLD FRIENDSHIPS

I spent a weekend recently with aunts, uncles, and cousins I had not seen in twelve years. It was wonderful. These people care about me. They are my roots. They know who I am and where I came from. They know the why of the me that is deep down inside.

Things are to be used. They have their time and place. When their time and place are gone they no longer matter. What really matters in the long run is people. The people who share our lives. The people who share our heritage. The people who share our earth.

That's what life is all about—caring for each other.

WALK YOUR
COFFEE BREAK

*T*ake a walk instead of a coffee break. Your body may need large-muscle activity more than it needs caffeine. Most of our bodies do.

Physical activity can be tiring, but it vents excess pressure. Walking is one of the most effective aerobic exercises and one that almost everyone can do. It also is a wonderful way to stimulate creative thinking. If you have some creative thinking to do, go walking. Get past that first mile or two and your mind will just go bananas with creative ideas and exciting things to think about. Walking can be a great deal of fun as well as great mental and physical stimulation.

THE DRIVER'S SEAT

*G*oals are essential to your personal and professional success. Without goals you can have no sense of purpose or direction in your life. Not having goals is like getting in your car, starting the engine, and never touching the steering wheel. You will definitely end up someplace, but it may not be where you intended. Not having goals is like spending all of your time planning your wedding and never planning your marriage, or spending all of your time planning your vacations and never planning your life.

Goals put you in control. They put you in the driver's seat of your life. Goals are very powerful. Try them! What do you have to lose?

Unclutter Your Life

*G*et rid of that stuff you never use—those clothes you never wear, those books that only sit on your shelf and are never read. Drop memberships in organizations that take more time than you have. Cancel subscriptions to magazines you no longer read. Unclutter your life. It will feel good.

CHECKLIST FOR TOMORROW

At the end of each day, before you leave your work area, make a list of the six most important things to do the next day and number them in the order of their importance. Each morning begin with the first item on your list and scratch it off when you are finished. Work your way right down the list. If you don't finish an item, put it on the list for the following day.

Bethlehem Steel paid thirty-five thousand dollars for this time-management idea. You may be surprised. It may be worth that much to you, too.

QUIET TIME

Establish uninterrupted "quiet time" each day to accomplish specific tasks. You will have to "make" this happen because it will not happen accidentally. You will find that two things quickly take place: (1) your production level will increase and (2) your stress level will decrease, because you are actually getting something done.

Use flextime to make it work. Cover for someone else and let that person cover for you. Go someplace else. I used to do this before I knew it was called "quiet time." I would periodically go down to a local pizza restaurant in the afternoon. I could get more work done there in two hours than I could all week in my office.

Use this in both your personal and professional life. It works!

IMPOSSIBLE PERFECTION

A perfectionist is someone who critiques not only the movie, but the popcorn and cokes as well.

It is impossible to be perfect. When you try, you set yourself up for failure. Every time you impose perfectionism on yourself or someone else, you cause undue stress. You are asking for an impossible task. Of course, you can do things perfectly if you try hard enough and long enough, but if you were perfect, you would do them perfectly every time.

On the other hand, you can be excellent every day. Contrary to popular belief, the word *excellent* does not mean perfect. Excellent means "your best." It means the best you can do right now, today, in this set of circumstances, with this knowledge and experience. If I give my best and have nothing more to give, I am excellent.

This does not mean that I can't grow. Of course I grow. A year from now when I work on a new book I expect it to be better than this one because I will have another year of knowledge and training and experience. But this one is excellent, because it is my best. And the new one will be excellent as well, because it, too, will be my best.

Enjoy being excellent every day!

REMEMBER HOW SPECIAL YOU ARE

Start—today—being the person you want to be, and believe that you can be that person. Remember how special you are—because you are. Walk your talk. Let people see that you believe in you.

Ninety-three percent of the way we communicate with other human beings is through non-verbal methods. Let people see how proud you are of you, because you have a right to be. Put a spring in your step and a song in your voice. Let the world know that you are happy to be here and that every day is a special day in your world. Proverbs says, "As he thinketh in his heart, so is he."

Believe in you, because

YOU ARE SPECIAL!

BE STILL

Sometimes I forget to be still.

As I was driving through Indiana last fall, I suddenly realized that I was in the most magnificent grove of fall trees I had ever seen. They were breathtaking. I wanted to stop and absorb every leaf. Sometimes I just want to watch the flowers grow, or sit on a rock and watch the water splash up on the beach. Life is so short and the days run by so rapidly. We have been given the blessing of living in this most gorgeous world, and we spend our time in such a rush that we miss it.

There's a scripture that says, "Be still and know that I am God." Have you been still lately?

KNOW YOUR PRIORITIES

*I*f I asked you right now what your top three priorities are, what would you say? You should be able to give me an instant answer. If you can't, you may want to spend some time thinking about them, because you need to know what they are.

Two very famous women in America, Mary Kay Ash, founder of Mary Kay Cosmetics, and author and speaker Rita Davenport, both say that their priorities are God first, family second, and job third. These may be very similar to your priorities or quite different. It really doesn't matter. But one thing they say applies to all of us. If our priorities are not in order, things will not go well in our lives. When your life seems just a little out-of-kilter, go back and look at your priorities.

SPLURGE!

Sometimes challenges seem to pile up. The stress level gets so high we wonder if anything beautiful will ever happen in our world again. Maybe we need to make it happen!

I had just gone through a period of successive crises and was feeling pretty low when our annual art festival started. I desperately needed a couple of hours of nondemanding time, so I went!

A beautiful hand-painted embossing of hearts jumped out at me. I don't know why I loved it. I just did. It made me feel happy. I needed that. So I splurged. I had never bought anything at the art festival before. That's okay. Sometimes we just need to splurge.

BACK BURNER

*P*ostpone thinking about problems. I am not talking about procrastination, but about the fact that sometimes, particularly when you are under a lot of stress, the most effective thing you can do may be to back away and give yourself a little time before you try to deal with the situation. This may be thirty minutes, half a day, or overnight. Give yourself a little time to get yourself under better control. Be good to you.

THINGS CAN CHANGE

I hear people say, "Things won't change. That is the way it has always been done. There is no reason to think about it." So what? Of course things can change! Of course we can change! It takes some courage and a lot of determination but changes can take place. Learn to test ideas rather than just accepting them. Ask questions. Evaluate. Make decisions for yourself based on your own information and best judgment. You are very capable and you have the wisdom of the world for your asking.

Be the person you were meant to be. Don't let anyone tell you that you can't do something because it has never been done. That's the time to begin.

77

ACT ENTHUSIASTIC

Don't save enthusiasm for special occasions. Use it now. Share it with everyone you meet. Enthusiasm comes from the Greek word *enthos*, which means "God within." Let the world see your inner beauty. Share enthusiasm with a friend.

COMPLIMENTS

ompliments are a lot of fun. They make you feel good and they make other people feel good. (Only sincere compliments, of course.) I love to walk through a hotel lobby or an airport, pay compliments, and just walk away.

Of course there is a trick to compliments. You must be able to receive them as well as give them. Only a person with very high self-esteem can both graciously give and receive compliments.

What do you say when you receive a compliment? "Thank you." That's it. Just "Thank you."

THIRTY-SECOND
RELAXATION

*P*eople tell me, "I do not have time to relax." Yes, you do. You may not choose to relax but you *can* make time to do so. You can relax in thirty seconds. For example, lean back and take some very slow, deep breaths. Close your eyes gently and say to yourself over and over again, "Relax, relax, relax."

Another quick method is to get comfortable and quickly envision yourself—in the greatest of detail—in a place where you feel very warm, peaceful, and secure.

Progressive muscle relaxation can also be accomplished in thirty seconds. Tighten all the muscles in your body and hold the tension for twenty to twenty-five seconds. Then let it go and shake it all out. The

tension will drain away from your body.

Relaxation is your choice. You may be like the man who leaned back, crossed his arms, and said, "I will do this, but I will not relax." The choice is yours.

STRETCH

*I*f you sit for an extended period of time, don't cross your legs. Periodically pull out the bottom drawer of your desk and put your foot up on it. It will relieve the pressure from the small of your back.

From time to time, get up and take a huge stretch. Stretching helps to relieve the stress in your entire body.

81

POSITIVE THOUGHTS

Control the amount of bad news you take in during any one day. If you have read the newspaper, maybe you don't want to listen to the radio or TV news. If you have listened to the news on the radio, maybe you don't want to watch the TV newscast that night.

Don't stick your head in the sand and ignore the world and its challenges, but be aware that you can only handle so much negative information at one time. As author and speaker Zig Ziglar says, "We live in a stinkin', thinkin', cat-kickin' world." We have to consciously put positive thoughts into our mind because the world is ready and willing to infiltrate our minds with negative information. Fortunately, our minds can hold only one thought at a time, either positive or negative. The choice is ours.

LISTEN TO YOUR BODY

After the Christmas holidays three or four years ago, I was under a lot of personal stress. We had had a lot of activity in our home for the holidays. We had just moved, and of course none of the decorations fit our new home. I was working on a doctoral dissertation, my father had had a heart attack, my father-in-law had an aneurysm, I had two teenagers living at home, and I had sixteen projects that had to be finished by April. I was very tired.

My body kept saying to me, "Donna, you are very tired, please get some rest." I said, "You don't understand. I have these projects to do and my dad is sick and I have these kids to take care of and I will have to rest later." Finally my body said, "I think we will have a cold." I said, "I don't have time to have a cold." We had a cold anyway, and it was thriving when flu season hit. My daughter became seriously ill with the flu and was taken to the hospital.

Now I had all the same stresses plus a cold and a child in the hospital. My body kept saying, "Donna, you are very tired, please get some rest." And I kept saying, "You don't understand." Finally, my body said, "I think we will have the flu." We had the flu. I got my rest. I had fever so high that I slept for days on end.

I look back now and think that if I had just listened to my body early in January and had taken a long weekend off, curled up in bed, watched TV, and eaten bonbons, I probably wouldn't have had either that cold or the flu.

Listen to your body. It will talk to you.

WHOOPS!

hoops! I made a mistake! Okay. So I made a mistake. The world is not going to come to an end. Don't take your mistakes too seriously. We all make a certain quota of them each day.

It is said that somewhere between one and three out of every ten decisions is usually dead wrong. But let's look at it a different way. This means that about 70 percent of our decisions are pretty close to being right. That's not too bad an average.

84

RIGHT NOW

*D*uring the day, stop and ask yourself: "Is there a better way, right now, for me to take care of me?" The answer to this question may be to relax your shoulders, take a walk, switch projects, throw away a leaky ballpoint pen, tackle something you have been putting off, have someone help you lift something, or maybe take a lunch break.

Be good to you. You deserve it.

CRY

Crying is a way of ridding the body of the stress chemicals found in emotional tears. I hear some men say, "I can't cry." Yes, you can! It takes a much stronger man to cry than to never cry.

Once, years ago, upon returning from a two-week vacation, I found that my house had a terrible odor. By the end of the week, I decided that we were either going to have to find the source of the odor or move out. There was obviously something dead or dying in the house and we could no longer stand it. I thought a mouse might have crawled under the refrigerator or freezer while we were gone and died, so I went out to check. As I got down on the floor to look under the freezer, I discovered that the carpet was wet and I thought, "Oh, no!" When I opened the

freezer door, I found that it had been out for approximately three weeks. I did have something dead and dying in the house. It was called beef and chicken and fish. The worst were the mashed bananas; they had exploded and created stalactites all over the freezer—rotten, mashed banana stalactites. It was awful!

What do you do when you have a crisis? You call your mother, right? I was a grown woman with half-grown children and my mother lived six hundred miles from me. I picked up the phone and tearfully told her what a mess I had. My mother is so wise, bless her heart. She listened very carefully and said, "Honey, I want you to sit down on the floor right where you are and I want you to cry and cry and cry. Then, when you get all through crying, get up and clean it up."

Pretty good advice. Sometimes we just need to cry it all out. Then, when it's all over, we get up and do what we can to solve the crisis.

IN THE MOMENT

*T*ake one day at a time and try to live in the present moment. We try to live yesterday, today, and tomorrow all at the same time. We can't do that. Yesterday is gone. Tomorrow is only a promissory note. All we have is today . . . right now. We need to learn to live one day and even one moment at a time because this is all we have. Nothing else is certain.

87

ASK YOURSELF . . .

"*I*n ten years, what difference is this going to make?"

This may help you keep things in perspective.

Think about it.

LEARNING ON THE ROAD

*T*he average person drives anywhere from 12,500 to 25,000 miles a year. If you break that down into hours, they equal one to two college semesters. During this time, you could be learning in your car.

While driving, listen to creative tapes. Listen to self-help tapes. Listen to your favorite music. Use this time creatively rather than spending it listening to "nothing" on the radio or to information that might cause you to think negatively.

When you are in charge of your mind, you are in control of your life.

CARRY A BOOK

*T*ake a book you would
like to read with you
at all times. If you get caught in
a traffic jam and have to sit for
a while, you will have something to read. If you arrive at
an appointment early or have
to wait, you will have something
to do that you enjoy.

You will have a greater
feeling of satisfaction for time
well used when you have chosen
how to use it.

SLEEP

*L*ack of sleep can make you more susceptible to stress and certainly more irritable. Yet the amount of sleep you require may be very different from that of others. Don't try to judge how much sleep or rest you should have based on someone else's needs. Get the amount that you, individually, need. You know your body better than anyone else. Listen to it.

CANDLELIGHT BUBBLE BATH

*T*ake a hot shower, bath, or sauna or sit in a whirlpool tub. Use whatever is available to you. Hot, moving water is a great way to relax.

Let's go even further. Take a candlelight bubble bath with a glass of wine. Or maybe you would rather do as I do: leave off the wine and listen to Christmas music. Now I know that it may not be the Christmas season, but that is what tapes are for. I love Christmas music so much that I keep some on tape so I can listen to it all year.

Enjoy!

PREPARE

Prepare the night before. Get your clothes ready. If you take your lunch, make it now. Lay out the items you are going to take with you: briefcase, papers, project. Straighten up your living areas so you will not have to do it in the morning. Make a list of things to do the next day. When you go to bed, you will be organized; if you happen to oversleep, you will not be so rushed and panic-stricken.

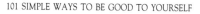

A GIFT FOR YOU

*B*uy a gift for yourself
for no reason at all.
Have it gift-wrapped and then
take your time unwrapping it.
Isn't that wonderful? Doesn't
it feel good? Besides, it is so
much fun.

94

TAKE A JOY BREAK

ometimes we just need to laugh. When situations get tense, take a joy break. Share a funny story with someone. Ask someone to share a funny story with you.

Keep a drawer or box with articles, jokes, and stories that tickle your funny bone. Your mind will work better and you will be much more productive when you laugh while you work.

SCREAM!

*P*ut a pillow over your face if you need to, but let it all out. Don't let all of that frustration build up inside of you. If you are in a place where you cannot scream, then go into the rest room or a private corner; jump up and down or run up and down a few flights of stairs. It won't take many flights before you are more concerned about breathing than you are about the current challenges in your life.

Pent-up emotions can do a great deal of physical damage to your body. Get them out.

LUNCH BREAK

*N*o matter how busy you are, take a lunch break. Whether you work in or out of your home, take a lunch break every day. Remove yourself both physically and mentally from your work area for at least fifteen minutes.

TAKE CARE OF YOU.

LEAVE YOUR WORK AT WORK

Some people leave their professional challenges on the doorstep as they walk into their home or hang them on a special tree in the yard. One man even planted a tree by his front door to leave his challenges on each night. When he went out the next morning, he would pick them up and take them back where they belonged.

Try not to take your professional concerns into your home, and don't take your personal or home concerns into your professional situation. Survival sometimes requires compartmentalizing our lives.

BACKUPS

Keep spare computer disks, car keys, house keys, an extra checkbook, an extra book of stamps, and a pile of parking meter change. If you have backups, you won't throw yourself into a stressful situation when you are running late and things are not going as smoothly as they could.

RELEARN
HOW TO PLAY

Sometimes we forget to play. Sometimes we forget *how* to play.

Go on a scavenger hunt. How long has it been since you did that? If it is raining, have a scavenger hunt at home. Go to the park and take crazy pictures of each other. Hold hands. Write a poem. Go walking in the rain.

Children run, they walk, they laugh, and they know how to play. Maybe we should watch them more often and relearn how to play.

COMEDY NIGHT

*W*atch old movies, TV, or VCR tapes. Enjoy them with a big bowl of popcorn. Just have a whole evening of popcorn and movies.

When you have had a particularly stressful week, rent funny movies because now is when you need to laugh.

Laughter is good medicine for the soul. Sometimes we have to LOOK for a reason to laugh.

101

SAY "I LOVE YOU"

My mother and father have been married for over sixty years. To commemorate their fiftieth anniversary, we had a big celebration.

I overheard a conversation that day they probably don't know I heard. Now you have to understand, my dad was a real "be strong" person, one of those people who loves very much but has always been taught to just be "strong." Mom and Dad were standing in the corner and I heard my mom say, "Do you love me?" My dad got this real shocked look on his face and said, "I told you I loved you the night I asked you to marry me. If I ever change my mind, I will let you know." I thought, "That's great, Dad. That was only fifty years ago!"

Sometimes we love people so much, but we hesitate to tell them. Those three words have

great depth of meaning, yet sometimes we just can't say them.

My dad loves me a great deal. I know that, but he doesn't say it. I miss that.

I love you, Dad.

P.S.: My dad passed away on my birthday, April 10, 1992. After having a stroke, he was finally able to say, in sign language, "I love you."

I miss you, Dad.

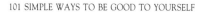

ACKNOWLEDGMENTS

My husband, Robert, has been a never-ending source of encouragement and support. He keeps the home fires burning while I'm away. My daughters, Tracey, Kristie, and Jennifer, have been great cheerleaders. My parents always told me I could be anything I wanted to be. Heartfelt thanks to my wonderful family for always believing in me.

Several people took time to read the draft manuscript and give their constructive comments. Special thanks for their ideas and encouragement go to:

Lahoma Bard
Pam Bommarito
Alta Campbell
Norma Church
Ginger Cuppett
Diana Deaton
Kay Duke
Michael English

Amy Harris
Clara Jean Jarman
Pamela Kern
Phyllis McConnell
Cindy Ottenbacher
Joe Vigil
Holly Whitten

Some very busy people took time to review the manuscript. Thank you to:

Judy "JT" Corley
Rita Davenport
Barbara Johnson
J. Terry Johnson
Florence Littauer

Beth Schwartz
Brian Tracy
Mark R. Truitt
Dennis Waitley
Joanne Wallace

for your special words of encouragement.

While I was on the road, the Bard Productions team made it all come together. Ray Bard got me started on this path and skillfully managed the process from beginning to end; Helen Hyams provided gentle, insightful editing; and Suzanne Pustejovsky made the words come alive with her text and cover design.

THE DONNA WATSON GROUP

The mission of The Donna Watson Group is to help people discover their own power and energy. Dr. Watson's presentations, whether keynote speeches or information-packed seminars, are known for their practical techniques and strategies. Her warm and witty style encourages people to think and grow—and to feel good about themselves.

Thousands of people from all types and sizes of organizations—including Fortune 500 corporations, growing companies, government agencies, and associations—have attended Donna's seminars. They include American Floral Service, General Motors, Emory University, International Paper, Kroger Foods, Motorola, Shawnee Indian Health Center, Tennaco, and the U.S. Marine Corps.

Donna's undergraduate degree is in education and her M.B.A. and Ph.D. degrees are in management. Her Ph.D. dissertation focused on stress management. In addition to authoring *101 Simple Ways to Be Good to Yourself*, Donna has recorded two six-tape albums, *Let Go and Live* on stress and self-esteem and *Winning Against Stress* on stress management.

For information about the services of The Donna Watson Group or to inquire about scheduling one of Donna's dynamic presentations, write or call:

The Donna Watson Group
1-800-945-3132

ORDER FORM

Quantity	Material	Total
	101 Simple Ways to Be Good to Yourself	
_____	Paperback edition, 128 pages, $7.95	_____
_____	Hardcover edition, 128 pages, $12.95	_____
_____	**Let Go and Live** (Six-tape album on self-esteem and stress management), $46.95	_____
_____	**Winning Against Stress** (Six-tape album on stress management with 30-page workbook), $54.95	_____
	Sales Tax (Texas residents only)	_____
	Shipping and handling	_____
	($2.00 for first book, $1.00 per book thereafter)	_____
	TOTAL	_____

**Quantity Discounts
are available.
Call
512-266-2112
for more information.**

☐ Please contact me about your workshops, presentations, and corporate seminars

Name _____

Organization _____

Address _____

City _____ State _____ Zip _____

Telephone (_____) _____

Please check one:
☐ MasterCard   ☐ VISA   Exp. Date _____

Card Number _____

Signature _____

Make checks payable to Energy Press. To order by phone, call 1-800-945-3132, or write to Energy Press, 5275 McCormick Mountain Drive, Austin, TX 78734.